One Wrld

THE HISTORY AND GOVERNMENT OF
THE UNITED STATES AND CANADA

J.M. Klein

PowerKiDS
press.

Published in 2021 by The Rosen Publishing Group, Inc.
29 East 21st Street, New York, NY 10010

First Edition

Editor: Caitie McAneney
Book Design: Seth Hughes

Photo Credits: Cover (top) f11photo/Shutterstock.com; cover (bottom) robbiepalmer92/Shutterstock.com; p. 5 Hulton Archive/Stringer/Getty Images; p. 6 Rischgitz/Stringer/Hulton Archive/Getty Images; p. 7 National Galleries of Scotland/Hulton Fine Art Collection/Getty Images; p. 8 Pierre5018/Wikimedia Commons; pp. 9, 22 Earthsound/Wikimedia Commons; p. 10 Mike Flippo/Shutterstock.com; p. 11 Hulton Archive/Staff/Getty Images; p. 14 (top) Allixpeeke/Wikimedia Commons; p. 14 (bottom) ZLEA/Wikimedia Commons; p. 15 (left) Skeezix1000/Wikimedia Commons; p. 15 (right) Ron Bull/Contributor/Toronto Star/Getty Images; p. 16 Hulton Archive/Stringer/Archive Photos/Getty Images; p. 17 Adam sk~commonswiki/Wikimedia Commons; pp. 18, 32 Bettmann/Contributor/Getty Images; p. 19 GraphicaArtis/Contributor/Archive Photos/Getty Images; pp. 20, 27 (top) Culture Club/Contributor/Hulton Archive/Getty Images; p. 21 Brendan Hoffman/Stringer/Getty Images News/Getty Images; p. 24 (left) Ted Russell/Contributor/The LIFE Images Collection/Getty Images; p. 24 (right) SesameStreetCred/Wikimedia Commons; p. 27 (bottom) Hulton Archive/Staff/Getty Images; p. 28 PHAS/Contributor/Universal Images Group/Getty Images; p. 29 DEA PICTURE LIBRARY/Contributor/De Agostini/Getty Images; p. 30 Edward Gooch Collection/Stringer/Hulton Archive/Getty Images; p. 31 Epics/Contributor/Hulton Archive/Getty Images; p. 33 Wolfgang Kaehler/Contributor/LightRocket/Getty Images; p. 34 Three Lions/Stringer/Hulton Archive/Getty Images; p. 35 DrRandomFactor/Wikimedia Commons; p. 37 gvictoria/Shutterstock.com; p. 38 Drew Angerer/Staff/Getty Images News/Getty Images; p. 39 Gino Santa Maria/Shutterstock.com; p. 40 Paul Thompson/Stringer/Hulton Archive/Getty Images; p. 41 -/Contributor/AFP/Getty Images; p. 42 (left) Larrybob/Wikimedia Commons; p. 42 (right) WayneRay/Wikimedia Commons; p. 44 Universal History Archive/Contributor/Universal Images Group/Getty Images.

Cataloging-in-Publication Data

Names: Klein, J.M.
Title: The history and government of the United States and Canada / J.M. Klein.
Description: New York : PowerKids Press, 2021. | Series: One world | Includes glossary and index.
Identifiers: ISBN 9781725321168 (pbk.) | ISBN 9781725321182 (library bound) | ISBN 9781725321175 (6 pack) | ISBN 9781725321199 (ebook)
Subjects: LCSH: United States–History–Juvenile literature. | United States–Politics and government–Juvenile literature.
Classification: LCC E178.3 K545 2021 | DDC 973–dc23

Manufactured in the United States of America

CPSIA Compliance Information: Batch #CSPK20: For Further Information contact Rosen Publishing, New York, New York at 1-800-237-9932

Find us on

CONTENTS

Introduction

THE **UNITED STATES** AND **CANADA**

Today, the United States and Canada are national examples of democracy, responsible for influencing governments and cultures around the world. For hundreds of years, people have **immigrated** to both countries for their representative democracies, hoping to be free from oppression and tyranny, and to have a voice in government.

The representative democracies of the United States and Canada share common roots. Both countries began as colonies, under the rule of other empires, and had to grow into the nations they are today. For the United States, that meant

representative democracy: A government in which citizens elect leaders to represent them in making decisions at different levels of government.

fighting the American Revolution from 1775 to 1783, throwing off the rule of a monarchy, and replacing the government with one that was led by the people instead of a king. For Canada, that meant a more gradual

From 1775 to 1783, former American colonists fought for independence against Great Britain in the American Revolution. General George Washington led the American troops and would later become the first president of the United States.

evolution toward independence. Canada transitioned from a colony to a country in 1867, but wasn't officially and completely independent from Great Britain until 1982.

Democracy was a radical idea back in the 1700s and 1800s. However, the basis for the colonists' revolutionary ideas already existed. The new experiment of the American government—and later the Canadian government—was the result of thousands of years of democratic ideas that date as far back as ancient Greece.

monarchy: A government ruled by one person with absolute power.

Chapter One

LIBERTY AND INDEPENDENCE

W hen the American Revolution ended in 1783, the former American colonies needed a new government. The American people had

The former thirteen American colonies declared independence from Britain in July 1776 with the signing of the Declaration of Independence, pictured here.

to grapple with what kind of country they wanted America to be—a nation with a strong central government or a nation of independent states. For the American Founding Fathers, every decision they made in forming the new government came down to one main goal—to avoid another tyrant.

British King George III ruled Great Britain from 1760 to 1820. The colonists considered King George a tyrant because he taxed the colonies without allowing them representation in Parliament.

In the lead-up to the revolution, King George III of Great Britain imposed a series of taxes to pay for the debt England incurred during the costly French and Indian War, a war that would also have a big impact on Canada. Britain also cracked down on American smuggling and

The Quebec Act of 1774 extended Canada's southern boundary to the Ohio River and granted French Canadian Catholics freedom of their religion. The act angered American colonists because it removed control of western land from the American colonies.

gave land to Canada in the 1774 Quebec Act, which angered American Protestants because it promised religious freedom to Quebec Catholics. While all of this was happening, the colonists didn't have a representative in Parliament.

History in F⬡CUS

Colonists in what was then Quebec did not join in the American Revolution, but remained loyal to the British crown. Besides being economically dependent on Britain, the Catholic Quebec colonists feared religious discrimination from primarily Protestant Americans.

"No taxation without representation" became the rallying cry of the revolutionaries, who believed that taxation without representation was "tyranny." Therefore, when

Parliament: The law-making body of England, now the United Kingdom.

the revolutionaries succeeded in removing King George, they sought to put measures in place to keep that from happening again.

For guidance, the Founding Fathers looked to an old English document called the Magna Carta, which limited the power of the king. That became the basis for limiting the power of the new American government. Under the U.S. Constitution, no single branch of government has the most authority.

THE MAGNA CARTA

No one is above the law—not even the king. That's the key principle of a document dating back to 1215, when it was signed by British King John.

· The Magna Carta—which means "great charter"—introduced the idea that the king does not have divine powers and that the law comes from the people to the king. Under the Magna Carta, the king could not imprison, take property from, or hurt his subjects—except by law. It became the foundation for jury trials and the rule of law.

Signed by King John in 1215, the Magna Carta gave British nobles more rights and limited the power of the king, establishing the idea that power comes from the people.

History in F◉CUS

The framers of the U.S. Constitution wanted to create a government that would not allow any one person to seize control–to become another king. King George III's rule was an **unlimited government**, where absolute power was given to a ruler and his appointees. Instead, the Founding Fathers created a **limited government**, where leaders were appointed by the people, and had limits to their power. Everyone– including authority figures like the president or prime minister–must follow the laws.

The preamble to the U.S. Constitution begins with "We the People," signifying that the American people have the right to participate in their government.

unlimited government: In an unlimited government, control is placed solely with the ruler and the ruler's appointees, and there are no limits on their authority.

ACHIEVING ENLIGHTENMENT

The ideas of revolution were informed by a period of time in the 18th century known as the Enlightenment—or the age of reason. Starting with "We the people," the U.S. Constitution signifies the people's right to choose the government, a foundational concept of the American political system. This concept of a social contract comes from Enlightenment-era thinkers. In a social contract, the state exists only to serve the will of the people, who are the source of all political power. People can choose to give or withhold this power. The Enlightenment's focus on reason also led to developing theories on limiting the power of government.

COMMON SENSE;

ADDRESSED TO THE

INHABITANTS

OF

A M E R I C A,

On the following interesting

S U B J E C T S.

I. Of the Origin and Design of Government in general, with concise Remarks on the English Constitution.

II. Of Monarchy and Hereditary Succession.

III. Thoughts on the present State of American Affairs.

IV. Of the present Ability of America, with some miscellaneous Reflections.

Man knows no Master save creating HEAVEN,
Or those whom choice and common good ordain.
THOMSON.

PHILADELPHIA;

Printed, and Sold, by R. BELL, in Third-Street,

MDCCLXXVI.

A pamphlet written by Thomas Paine called Common Sense *advocated for American independence from Great Britain. It also reflected ideas from the Enlightenment, such as reason and natural human rights.*

---

limited government: In a limited government led by the citizens, everyone, including all authority figures, must obey the laws.

History in F◉CUS

Democratic republics, as in the United States and Canada, are governments where power comes from the people through elections. Monarchies and dictatorships, as in North Korea, are governments where one person has all the power. Oligarchies, as in China, are governments where a small group has all the power.

Today the United States—along with Canada—remains a government with rule by many, where the people have the power to shape their government. Limited governments help protect human rights, ensure opportunities for all citizens, and encourage economic freedom—just as the Founding Fathers wanted.

Chapter Two

NATION BUILDERS

After gaining independence from Great Britain, the American Founding Fathers didn't want a government that was too powerful. That was the entire reason they had rebelled. Fearing a strong central government, the Second Continental Congress set out to create a new government that was deliberately weak. In 1777, the Articles of Confederation became the first constitution of the United States, and it established a loose system of **sovereign**, independent states. Each of the states had an equal vote, despite their population. The new country did not have a president and Congress had limited power.

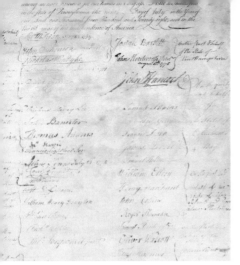

The Articles of Confederation was the United States' short-lived first constitution, which resulted in a national government that proved to be too weak.

Money printed by the Continental Congress was essentially worthless, one of the many reasons the Founding Fathers decided to start over with a new constitution.

But the Articles of Confederation ended up being too weak and the new country ran into problems. The government—known as the Continental Congress—had no power of national taxation, a $42 million debt from the American Revolution, and it couldn't control trade. The money issued by the Continental Congress was essentially worthless. Seven of the thirteen states printed their own paper money, which wasn't accepted outside of that state. The Continental Congress also couldn't control trade, which meant that some states charged fees on goods brought in from other states. Also, there was no national court system.

INDEPENDENCE FOR CANADA

The path to Canadian independence was a gradual one. Short-lived rebellions in 1837 and 1838 spread public support for Canadian independence and forced Great Britain to compromise and allow for some self-rule.

In 1867, England united the colonies of Canada, Nova Scotia, and New Brunswick into the Dominion of Canada in the Constitution Act. Canada could act like its own country with its own laws and parliament, and had financial independence. However, Canada was still under British rule. It would not gain full legal freedom until the Statute of Westminster in 1931. Canada became completely independent and adopted its own constitution in 1982.

AN ACT

OF THE IMPERIAL PARLIAMENT

FOR THE

UNION

OF

CANADA, NOVA SCOTIA AND
NEW BRUNSWICK,

The 1867 Canada Constitution Act created the Dominion of Canada by uniting the colonies of Canada, Nova Scotia, and New Brunswick. Under this constitution, Canada could act like its own country.

Queen Elizabeth II of Great Britain signs a proclamation in 1982 that allows Canada to create its own constitution and become fully independent.

General George Washington presides over the Constitutional Convention in 1787. The Founding Fathers met to amend the Articles of Confederation but instead decided to scrap the Articles and start over with a new constitution.

American leaders met to amend the Articles of Confederation at the Constitutional Convention in 1787. Instead, they started over with a new constitution.

The framers of the Constitution had to decide how to distribute power—whether it should be concentrated or shared among the states. Some, like Alexander Hamilton, were strongly in favor of a strong central government, almost to the degree of a unitary system. Under a unitary system of government, one central national government makes decisions that affect all parts of a country and performs all government functions.

History in F⊙CUS

Alexander Hamilton, James Madison, and John Jay wrote a series of 85 essays called *The Federalist Papers*, which urged ratification of the U.S. Constitution. Those essays helped explain the decision to split power between the national and state governments.

unitary: Relating to or forming a single unit.

James Madison, the "father of the Constitution," pitched the idea that the Virginia constitution was based on. Under its new constitution, the United States would follow a federalist model. States would share powers and function with a powerful central government. A central government would not take power from the states but could make laws that affect how the states govern.

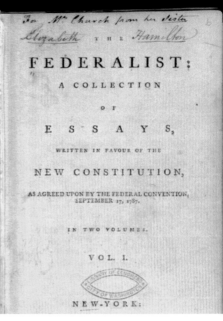

The Federalist Papers were a series of essays written to defend the U.S. Constitution and explain the decision for dividing the powers of government between the national and state governments.

AIMING FOR AUTONOMY

The aftermath of World War I had an impact on Canada's desire to self-govern its own affairs. As a part of the British Commonwealth, Canadians did not choose to join the war but sent soldiers as requested. Almost 61,000 Canadian soldiers died in the war, the most in Canadian history. A growng sense of national pride in the accomplishment of their soldiers plus a desire for **autonomy** led to the Statute of Westminster in 1931. Canada gained full legal freedom and equal standing with England and other Commonwealth countries.

federalist: Relating to or supporting a strong federal government.

Federalism also shaped Canada's government. Power is divided between the central government based in Ottawa and the ten Canadian provinces.

United States President Franklin Roosevelt signs the law known as The New Deal in 1933. The New Deal provided grants and programs to help get the United States out of the Great Depression, evolving the role of federalism.

History in F⚙CUS

During the American Great Depression in the 1930s, President Franklin Roosevelt's New Deal changed the role of federalism in the United States. Roosevelt introduced cooperative federalism. The national government encouraged state and local governments to work on national goals through grants and fines.

Chapter Three

DIVISION OF
POWER

Both the Canadian and U.S. governments are divided into three branches–legislative, executive, and judicial.

The main job of the legislative branch is to make laws. The executive branch is in charge of executing the laws. And the judicial branch, the courts, interprets the laws and explains what they mean.

This artwork shows the framers of the U.S. Constitution at the Constitutional Convention of 1787. The constitution was ratified, or signed, in 1788.

The Roman Senate is assembled in a temple in this illustration. The Senate was one of three branches of the Roman Republic's government.

The United States and Canada both have bicameral legislative systems, which means that the lawmaking body of government is two separate houses or chambers. The United States Congress's two-house system includes the House of Representatives and the Senate.

History in F☉CUS

The early Roman Republic divided government into three parts— the consuls, the Senate, and the Assembly. These three branches were the executive, legislative, and judicial branches of the Roman Republic, and the origin of the idea of checks and balances.

The Senate is made up of two elected senators from each state, while the number of state members in the House of Representatives

bicameral: Having two parts; used to describe a government in which the people who make laws are divided into two groups.

is based on the population of each state. States with a large population, like California, have a high number of representatives in the House of Representatives, while states with a smaller population, like Alaska, can have as few as one.

The U.S. House of Representatives is one of the two houses of the United States' bicameral legislative system. The number of members in the House of Representatives is capped at 435. There are currently 100 senators in the Senate.

The American people elect the president of the United States using a system called the electoral college. The key difference between the United States and Canada's governments is that in Canada, the legislative branch has authority over—and chooses—the executive branch.

THE GREAT COMPROMISE

When the U.S. Constitution was being written, the framers couldn't agree on what kind of legislature to have. Delegates from larger populations wanted the Virginia Plan's proportional representation. The legislature would be chosen based on the state's population so that larger states would have more legislators and more power. States with smaller populations wanted the New Jersey Plan's equal representation so that they would have equal power in Congress.

Connecticut's Roger Sherman came up with "The Great Compromise." The country would have two houses—one with equal power, one with proportional power. Dividing the legislature would also ensure it didn't have too much power, another form of checks and balances.

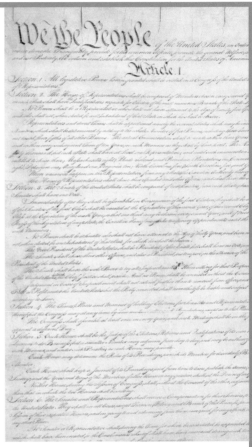

The U.S. Constitution is the supreme law of the land, which means no state can create a law that goes against it. But it's also a "living document." It can be amended so that it stays flexible.

Canada has what is called a parliamentary system, which is based off of the British parliamentary system. The Canadian Parliament is also divided into two chambers–the House of Commons and the Senate. The House of Commons is elected, but the Senate is not. The 105 members of the Senate are appointed by the current or previous prime minister and serve until the age of 75.

History in F⦿CUS

Canada is still part of the British Commonwealth and is a constitutional monarchy, where the British monarch is the head of state. Queen Elizabeth II of Great Britain became the queen of Canada in 1952, but her powers are only symbolic.

Canada's House of Commons is made up of 338 representatives known as Members of Parliament, who are elected to represent the 338 Canadian communities. The political party with the most Members of Parliament forms the government of Canada and picks the prime minister of Canada.

Chapter Four

TAXES, CHOICES, AND ECONOMICS

In the 17th and 18th centuries, an intensive rivalry developed between the British, French, and Spanish empires, who fought for global dominion through the colonization of North America. The colonies were seen as a way of enriching the home country—and trade was regulated accordingly.

The dominant economic theory of the time was the idea of **mercantilism**. Leaders in Britain, France and Spain believed that there was a limited amount of wealth in the world and that countries had to compete as much as possible to acquire that wealth. To achieve that, those

colonization: The act of making or establishing a settlement in a new territory that maintains ties to a distant parent state.

leaders believed that government policy should be set up so that a country exported as much as possible and imported as little as possible.

Colonies would sell raw materials, which were sent to the home country and manufactured, then sent back to the colonies and sold as finished goods. The colonists were banned from competing with manufacturers in the home country.

British colonists in America exported raw materials like tobacco or rice in exchange for luxury items from England like nicer clothes or eyeglasses. From the 1650s to the 1760s, the Navigation Acts regulated and taxed American trade. Laws required colonists to trade only with English ships—and only from a list

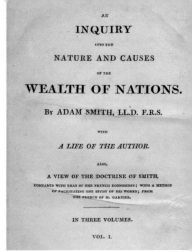

Adam Smith's The Wealth of Nations argued against the theory of mercantilism. Smith is known as the father of modern-day economics.

American colonists provided raw materials like tobacco, which they sent to Great Britain to be manufactured, and Great Britain then returned to the colonies to be sold as finished goods.

History in F◉CUS

In 1776, Scottish philosopher Adam Smith upended the mercantilist system with his work, *The Wealth of Nations*. Smith argued that allowing people to act in their own "self interest" would mean open markets and competition—creating more wealth for everyone.

of approved goods. This was to prevent a colonial market forming for goods Britain might not be able to provide. The colonies were also forbidden from exporting goods directly to other countries. Laws like the Molasses Act in 1733 banned New England merchants from buying French sugar to make rum.

When the French and Indian War left Britain in severe debt, they imposed

American colonists protested the Stamp Act, one of several taxes imposed by Great Britain to help raise revenue to pay off debt from the costly French and Indian War.

new tariffs and taxes to help collect revenue, or income. Those included the Sugar, Stamp, and Townshend Acts, which taxed sugar, newspapers, legal documents, oil, and tea. Aware of the colonies' thriving smuggling operation, Britain also sent royal customs officials to make sure taxes were being collected and to catch illegal imports.

FREE TRADE

Freed from British taxes and regulations, the new American nation developed a free trade system. Americans could now buy and make goods as they wished.

The new unlimited government of the United States followed a free enterprise system. American businesses are free from government control and operate under a minimal amount of government regulations. Prices go up or down because of supply and demand, not because the government sets them. Private companies compete for profit without the government interfering.

Canada follows similar economic policies today, except the Canadian government plays a larger role than the United States in regulating and **subsidizing** Canadian industries.

In this painting, the British surrender at the Battle of Saratoga in 1777, leaving the United States free to form its own economic policies.

free enterprise: An economic system characterized by freedom for consumers and producers.

Boston colonists dressed as Native Americans boarded British ships and threw tea overboard as a protest against Great Britain's taxes during the Boston Tea Party.

In 1773, the colonists rebelled by boycotting British products and then raiding British ships and throwing tea overboard, an event that became known as the Boston Tea Party. Great Britain pushed back harder, and mercantilist regulations on trade ultimately sparked the American Revolution.

History in F⚙CUS

New ideas of liberty changed the American economy by leading to a decline in work by **indentured servants** and **apprentices**. And after the American Revolution, there was a clear split between the North, which shifted to paid labor, and the South, where slave labor dominated.

THE NATIONAL DEBT

The United States racked up a large national debt during the expensive American Revolution, as did many of the individual states. Following the war, the Founding Fathers had to figure out how to pay the debt.

Alexander Hamilton believed the United States could become a strong manufacturing nation while Thomas Jefferson saw the United States as a nation of independent farmers. Hamilton and Jefferson reached a compromise in 1790. The national government would take over and pay for the states' debt by consolidating state debt into a national debt. That would create national credit. In return, the nation's capital would be moved to the American South in the District of Columbia.

Alexander Hamilton was the first secretary of the U.S. Treasury, and created the First Bank of the United States in 1791.

Chapter Five

NATIONS OF MANY CULTURES

From their start as colonies, the United States and Canada have been nations of immigrants. Large numbers of immigrants came to both countries during the colonial era as countries fought for dominion over different parts of North America. Immigration continued in waves throughout the centuries as people came to the United States and Canada seeking religious freedom and economic opportunities.

Ellis Island near New York City was the main immigration center for the United States. Because of that, New York became a very diverse and populated city.

INDIGENOUS PEOPLES

The United States and Canada were home to indigenous people for thousands of years before settlers arrived, with unique cultures and histories. White settlers decimated the indigenous population by enslaving and killing native people, and introducing new diseases. They also removed indigenous people from their land and forced them to live on reservations.

In both countries, a significant number of indigenous tribes still keep their traditional cultures alive. In the United States, 573 American Indian and Alaska Native tribes are recognized, with 5.2 million members. Some 1.6 million indigenous people, or First Nations, live in Canada. There are 634 First Nation tribes, speaking more than 50 languages.

Millions of American Indians and First Nations peoples live in the United States and Canada today and maintain traditional cultures. They are not one big culture, but instead, each tribe or nation has its own customs, traditions, and histories.

indigenous: Describing groups that are native to a particular region.

Today that means that both nations have great diversity of culture, language, and religion. Canada was the first country in the world to adopt multiculturalism as official government policy in 1971. Canada has one of the highest per capita immigration admission rates in the world and leads the world in refugee resettlement. Today, migrants from all over the world make their home in Canada and the United States.

Some of North America's first settlers came to the "New World" to escape religious persecution. In 1620, a Separatist Puritan religious group we now call "Pilgrims" fled England and established a colony in Plymouth, Massachusetts. Nearly 1,000 Puritans also sought religious freedom by forming the Massachusetts Bay Colony shortly after in 1630.

Many early American settlers came to the United States fleeing religious persecution. In 1620, a group of around 100 Separatists Puritans landed in what's now Plymouth Rock, Massachusetts.

diversity: Exhibiting a variety of types.

multiculturalism: The preservation of different cultures or cultural identities within a unified society.

FRENCH-CANADIAN QUÉBÉCOIS

Founded in 1608 by French settlers, the Canadian province of Quebec is still **francophone**—or French speaking—today. Around 81 percent of the Québécois speak French. English speakers in Quebec are a minority.

While both French and English are the official languages of Canada, outside of Quebec, English is the most commonly spoken language. Because of the cultural and language divide, the French-Canadian Québécois have considered separating from the rest of Canada, especially during the 1960s. In 1980 and 1995, **referendums** asked Quebec voters if they wanted to officially leave Canada. Both times Quebec voted to stay a part of Canada.

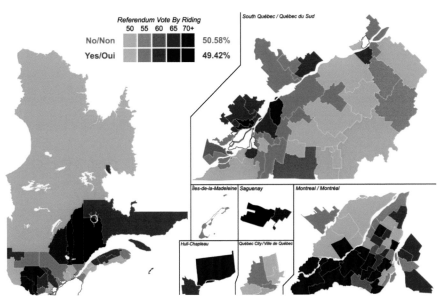

French-Canadian Quebec residents have considered separating from the rest of Canada. This map shows how people voted to stay a part of the country in the 1995 referendum.

migrant: Someone who moves from one region to another.

Québécois: A French-speaking native or inhabitant of Quebec.

35

Today, both the Canadian and the U.S. constitutions protect freedom of religion and seek to keep religion separate from government. Christianity is the dominant religion, but the United States and Canada are home to many diverse religions. Later immigrants were seeking a better life, including 4.5 million Irish immigrants, who arrived between 1820 and 1930 to escape a famine in Ireland.

History in F⬡CUS

More than 27 million people immigrated to the United States between 1880 and 1930. Most of those immigrants came from western Europe, but immigrants also came from the Middle East, the Mediterranean, and southern and eastern Europe.

Other people came to America against their will. From the 1500s to 1800s, an estimated 12.5 million Africans were brought to the New World—North America, South America, and the Caribbean—and those who survived were sold into slavery. Black or African American citizens now make up about 12 percent of the population of the United States.

History in F◉CUS

Immigrants could come to the United States without any restrictions—until 1882. That's when the U.S. government passed the Chinese Exclusion Act, banning Chinese laborers from coming to America. Around 25,000 Chinese people migrated to California during the 1850s California gold rush.

Because of its background as a former British colony, English has historically been the main language spoken by Americans. However, the United States does not have an official language. Colonists in the former American colonies spoke English, Dutch, German, and French. Today around 350 languages are spoken across the country.

Spanish as a language is expected to grow in usage in the United States as the Latino community increases. Today there are around 41 million native Spanish speakers in the United States.

Spanish is the second most popular language spoken in the United States today. As the number of Spanish-speaking immigrants to the United States grows, the Spanish language is growing in use.

The Statue of Liberty historically welcomed immigrants to the United States as they arrived on Ellis Island. The statue's torch is said to light the way to freedom.

Chapter Six

DEMOCRACY
IN ACTION

While the American revolutionaries embraced ideas of freedom and equality, those rights were saved for white men. Slaves were excluded from the U.S. Constitution, which valued them as only three-fifths of a person for the purpose of counting state representation in federal government. Women didn't have the right to vote or own property for a long time after the United States was born.

Voting is a civic responsibility in both Canada and the United States. However, only about 61 percent of eligible voters participated in the 2016 U.S. presidential election.

It took civic effort to change these injustices. **Abolitionists** fought for the end of slavery, which in 1868 was finally outlawed with the Fourteenth Amendment to the U.S.

In this photograph, women's suffrage supporters march in a parade. It took civic involvement to give women the right to vote in the United States.

amendment: A change or addition to a constitution.

Constitution. The woman's suffrage moment fought for the right for women to vote, finally achieving it with the passage of the Nineteenth Amendment in 1920. It would take the 1950s and 1960s American civil rights movement, an organized effort by black Americans to end racial discrimination, for black Americans to gain equal protection under the law. Those **activists** participated in civic causes to make the United States a more just place for everyone.

Dr. Martin Luther King Jr. waves to a crowd gathered for the March on Washington at the National Mall in 1963. It took organized involvement for black Americans to gain equal protection under the law.

PROTECTION OF RIGHTS

American and Canadian citizens have rights that are protected by the constitution of each country. In the United States., the Bill of Rights makes up the first ten amendments to the U.S. Constitution. The Canadian Charter of Rights and Freedoms begins Canada's 1982 Constitution.

These bills of rights provide personal, political, and economic protections. Canadians' and Americans' personal rights include the right to live without discrimination based on race, national origin, sex, or religion. Political rights ensure the right to speak, petition, assemble, vote, and publish freely. Citizens also have economic rights. They can own property, join a union, change employment, or start a business.

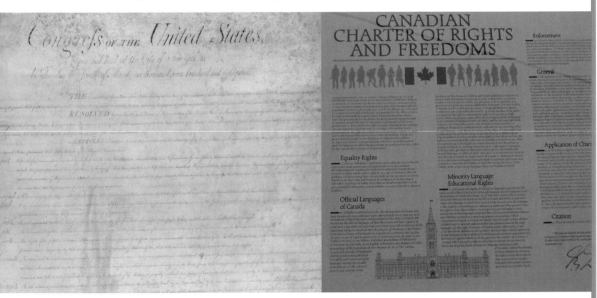

The U.S. Bill of Rights is the first ten amendments to the U.S. Constitution. It protects the rights of American citizens, including rights to free speech, liberty, property, and free exercise of religion.

The Canadian Charter of Rights and Freedoms is the first part of Canada's 1982 Constitution and serves as the Canadian bill of rights.

American and Canadian citizens have many rights, but they also have civic responsibilities. They must participate in their government; that's how representative democracies work. Protecting civil liberties requires citizens to be activists—and to be aware of the ways the government might be unjust for some. It's vital for people who are in the majority to pay attention to the civil rights of others, especially minorities.

History in F◉CUS

Enlightenment philosophers like John Locke valued "natural rights" such as life, liberty, and property. Thomas Jefferson expanded on this idea when he listed life, liberty, and the pursuit of happiness as "unalienable rights" given to everyone in the Declaration of Independence.

One major civic responsibility in a representative democracy is to vote. At the age of 18, citizens can vote in both the United States and Canada to have their voices heard. Citizens should pay attention to the actions of

CIVIC RESPONSIBILITIES

Civic responsibilities go back to ancient Rome. Roman Republic elections were more limited than those we have today. In ancient Rome, officials were chosen only from patricians, or nobles.

When the plebeians—or commoners— felt their rights were hampered in favor of the patricians, Roman commissioners created the Twelve Tables. Posted in the Roman Forum, the Twelve Tables informed plebeians of the law and helped protect their rights.

Posting the Twelve Tables introduced equality before the law. All Roman citizens—regardless of status—were held equally accountable to the law. They were also innocent until proven guilty and were tried by a jury of peers.

The Twelve Tables were a set of laws written on tablets in ancient Rome in 451 and 450 BC so that the commoners would know their rights.

elected leaders at all levels–local, state, and federal. They can even communicate with leaders through phone calls, letters, and petitions.

People can practice good citizenship in their everyday actions. They can get involved in their community, do charity work, and serve in the armed forces. Other examples of good citizenship

History in F●CUS

Responsibilities are different from duties. Paying taxes, obeying laws, and serving on a jury are civic duties, or things people *have* to do. If citizens don't do these things, they might be punished with jail time or fines.

include going to school and taking responsibility for one's actions. Above all, a good citizen always respects the rights of other people. Citizenship keeps democratic institutions in the United States and Canada alive and thriving.

institution: A significant practice, relationship, or organization in a society or culture.

GLOSSARY

abolitionist: One who fights to end slavery.

activist: One who acts strongly in support of or against an issue or cause; a person who uses or supports strong actions to help make changes in politics or society.

apprentice: A person who learns a job or skill by working for a fixed period of time for someone who is very good at that job or skill.

autonomy: The quality or state of being self-governing.

francophone: Having French as the main language.

immigrate: To come to a country to live there.

impeach: To charge with misconduct in office.

indentured servant: A person required by a contract to work for a certain period of time.

mercantilism: The economic theory that trade increases wealth, and a nation should export more than it imports for profit.

referendum: A public vote on a particular issue.

sovereign: Having independent authority and the right to govern itself.

subsidize: To help someone or something pay for the costs of something.

veto: An act of one branch of a government forbidding or prohibiting the carrying out of projects attempted by another branch.

FOR MORE INFORMATION

BOOKS:

Brennan Demuth, Patricia. *What Is the Constitution?* New York, NY: Penguin Random House, 2018.

Harris, Michael. C. *What Is the Declaration of Independence?* New York, NY: Penguin Random House, 2016.

Rothman, Lily. *Everything You Need to Ace American History in One Big Fat Notebook: The Complete Middle School Study Guide.* New York, NY: Workman Publishing Co., 2016.

WEBSITES:

Canada's History for Kids
kids.canadashistory.ca/Kids/Home.aspx
Games, contests, and videos are featured on this website focusing on Canadian history.

Crash Course
thecrashcourse.com/courses/ushistory
Crash Course features dozens of easy-to-understand and humorous videos explaining U.S. history and government.

National Constitution Center
constitutioncenter.org/interactive-constitution
The National Constitution Center offers an interactive website to analyze the U.S. Constitution.

INDEX